BOB
'15-'16

W9-BSD-843

WILD ANIMAL NEIGHB🐾RS

SHARING OUR URBAN W🐾RLD

ANN DOWNER

TWENTY-FIRST CENTURY BOOKS / MINNEAPOLIS

ACKNOWLEDGMENTS

Stephen DeStafano of the University of Massachusetts, Amherst, and USGS Massachusetts Cooperative Fish & Wildlife Research Unit got me interested in urban wildlife when we worked together on *Coyote at the Kitchen Door: Living with Wildlife in Suburbia* (2011), his book for grown-ups. While researching my own book on elephant communication, I became interested in human-wildlife conflict around the globe and the many forms it could take in our increasingly urbanized world.

The following people were extremely generous with their time and knowledge. Any errors that remain in the book are my own. *Raccoons:* Andrew N. Iwanuik, University of Lethbridge; Suzanne McDonald, York University. *Mountain lions:* Ryan Phillips, Ryan Bourbour, and Breanna Martinico, De Anza College Environmental Studies Department; Seth Riley and Jeff Sikich, Santa Monica Mountains National Recreation Area, National Park Service. *Crows:* Midori Yanagihara. *Coyotes:* Heidi Garbe, Max McGraw Wildlife Foundation; Stanley D. Gehrt, the Ohio State University and the Cook County, Illinois, Coyote Project; Warren Fahey. *Alligators:* Kent A. Vleit, University of Florida; Amos Cooper, Texas Parks and Wildlife; Louise Hayes-Odum. *Loggerhead sea turtles:* Linda Soderquist; Zander Srodes; Jean Srodes. *Gray-headed flying foxes:* Nick Edards; Batwatch Australia.

I'm also grateful to the vast network of scholars and citizen scientists behind three online resources that made the task of fact-checking various aspects of the animals' life histories much simpler: The Encyclopedia of Life, Animal Diversity Web, and ARKive.

Two nature documentaries produced by Susan K. Fleming, *Raccoon Nation* and *A Murder of Crows*, provided invaluable insights.

TITLE PAGE: AN ALLIGATOR CROSSES A FLOODED ROADWAY NEAR GALVESTON, TEXAS.

Twenty-First Century Books
A division of Lerner Publishing Group, Inc.
241 First Avenue North
Minneapolis, MN 55401 USA

For reading levels and more information, look up this title at www.lernerbooks.com.

Library of Congress Cataloging-in-Publication Data

Downer, Ann, 1960–
    Wild animal neighbors : sharing our urban world / by Ann Downer.
     p. cm
    Includes bibliographical references and index.
    ISBN 978–0–7613–9021–3 (library binding : alkaline paper)
    ISBN 978–1–4677–1663–5 (eBook)
    1. Urban animals—Juvenile literature. 2. Urban ecology—Juvenile literature. 3. City and town life—Juvenile literature. 4. Suburban life—Juvenile literature. 5. Human-animal relationships—Juvenile literature. 6. Nature—Effect of human beings on—Juvenile literature. I. Title.
QH541.5.C6D69 2014
591.75'6—dc23   2012043817

Manufactured in the United States of America
2 – PC – 2/1/14

CONTENTS

THE BEAR IN THE BACKYARD

I LIVE IN SOMERVILLE, MASSACHUSETTS, ACROSS THE RIVER FROM BOSTON. IN THIS CITY OF SEVENTY-FIVE THOUSAND PEOPLE, THE HOUSES ARE PACKED TIGHTLY TOGETHER— BUT NOT TOO TIGHT FOR WILDLIFE. My backyard has been visited by raccoons, opossums, woodchucks, rabbits, bats, hawks, snakes, and skunks. A coyote has walked the former railroad bed that runs behind our house.

So far, no bears.

But on May 26, 2012, about two hours from my home, a young black bear was spotted in Provincetown on Cape Cod. By June the bear was a celebrity, with many local sightings in cranberry bogs and on a golf course. People across New England and across the country followed the bear's exploits on YouTube and Twitter.

On June 12, the Massachusetts Environmental Police darted the bear and transported it off the Cape. But that wasn't the end of the bear's story.

Two weeks after his Cape Cod vacation, the bear was back, this time in a suburb of Boston. The state's Large Animal Response Team found the bear up a tree in the wealthy neighborhood of Chestnut Hill. For the second time in two weeks, the young male was darted. This time, he was released in the western part of the state.

For many New Englanders, the Cape Cod bear came to symbolize the problem of urban wildlife: a wild animal that strays out of the wild into human suburbs and cities. We are asking ourselves: What is bringing these creatures out of the wild and into our paved-over, glassed-in, and built-up human habitats, our concrete jungles? And once here, why do they stay? What does it mean to be "urban" or "wild" in the twenty-first century? In the chapters that follow, we will visit city sidewalks and suburban backyards the world over to find out.

THE CAPE COD BEAR WAS A PERSISTENT VISITOR IN URBAN AREAS OF EASTERN MASSACHUSETTS IN THE SPRING AND SUMMER OF 2012. HERE, HE PERCHES IN A TREE IN THE CHESTNUT HILL NEIGHBORHOOD OF BROOKLINE, A SUBURB OF BOSTON.

BLACK BEAR FACTS

Despite their common name, black bears can be brown, cinnamon, or blond. In Alaska they even have cream or blue-gray coats. While they mostly eat roots, berries, and insects, black bears quickly acquire a taste for human food. Using their powerful claws like can openers, they can even get into locked vehicles.

SCIENTIFIC NAME: *Ursus americanus*

ALSO KNOWN AS: American black bear

RELATED TO: The black bear shares its genus, *Ursus,* with the brown or grizzly bear and the polar bear.

SIZE: Males range from 55 to 79 inches (1.4 to 2 meters) long and weigh from 110 to more than 800 pounds (about 50 to 400 kilograms). Females are shorter and lighter, from 47 to 63 inches (1.2 to 1.6 m) long and between 86 and 520 pounds (about 40 to 250 kg).

NATIVE TO NORTH AMERICA: Yes. Black bears are found from Canada southward as far as northern Mexico.

ENDANGERED: No (Black bears are listed by the International Union for the Conservation of Nature as a Species of Least Concern.)

CITY AS ECOSYSTEM

Wild things survive and even thrive in our cities and suburbs. Many aren't just passing through. They call the city home. Some, like weeds and rats, pigeons, and bedbugs, have been city dwellers since the time of the earliest cities. Others have found a home in the city as their wild habitat shrinks and disappears. Here are some of the features that make the urban ecosystem unique.

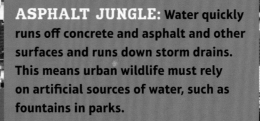

ASPHALT JUNGLE: Water quickly runs off concrete and asphalt and other surfaces and runs down storm drains. This means urban wildlife must rely on artificial sources of water, such as fountains in parks.

ARTIFICIAL LIGHT: Cities never sleep. Artificial light creates a permanent glow over urban areas and can disrupt the sleeping and waking cycles of people and wildlife alike.

HEAT ISLANDS: Cities are warmer than surrounding country or wilderness. Scientists call this the heat island effect. The warmer city is a more appealing place for some animals, such as raccoons, to raise a family.

STEEL AND GLASS: The way sound bounces off the surfaces of buildings is causing some city birds to alter their songs to be heard.

GREEN SPACES: Most plants in cities are nonnative, and grass and trees are clipped, pruned, and artificially maintained. Plant-eating animals aren't able to find wild foods. Urban wildlife can be sickened by pesticides used on urban green spaces.

ARTIFICIAL CLIFFS: Skyscrapers provide habitat for cliff-nesting species, such as hawks and swallows.

CHAPTER 1

THE RACCOON IN THE TRASH CAN

ANYTOWN, U.S.A.

WHEN YOU THINK OF WILD ANIMALS INVADING THE BACKYARD, WHAT IS THE FIRST IMAGE THAT COMES TO MIND? IF YOU LIVE IN NORTH AMERICA, CHANCES ARE IT'S THE FAMILIAR MASKED FACE BELOW. Raccoons are a nuisance. They raid our garbage cans, come through pet doors to snack from the cat's dish, or snatch a pizza from the kitchen counter when our backs are turned. We worry that they might carry rabies. But at the same time, raccoons are, well, pretty adorable.

How did raccoons come to be the familiar creatures raiding our garbage cans? Raccoons probably got used to human beings well before Europeans came to the Americas. The word *raccoon* is borrowed from the native Powhatan word *raugroughcun*. By the time settlers began cutting down forests to plant crops, the raccoon was already accustomed to raiding the garbage piles on the edge of villages—perhaps even stealing fish from the fish traps the Powhatan set in local streams.

In the wild, a raccoon will claim a home range. It will patrol this territory, looking for food and mates, and defend it against other raccoons. It may make several dens throughout its home range, often using the former burrows of foxes or woodchucks or a hollow tree.

IN THE WILD, RACCOONS WILL SOMETIMES FIGHT OVER TASTY TREATS SUCH AS BIRD EGGS. IN THE CITY, THEY WILL OFTEN FIGHT OVER HUMAN FOOD SUCH AS DOUGHNUTS AND FRENCH FRIES.

RACCOONS ARE MOST ACTIVE AT NIGHT. THEY ARE EXTREMELY AGILE AND HAVE NO TROUBLE GETTING INTO GARBAGE BINS, EVEN IF THE LID IS ON, TO SCAVENGE FOR FOOD.

RACCOON
FACTS

This familiar mammal is the most common and widespread medium-sized carnivore in North America. Since raccoons drink and forage near water, a permanent source of water is necessary for them to survive, whether they live in the city or the country.

SCIENTIFIC NAME: **Procyon lotor**

ALSO KNOWN AS: Common raccoon, northern raccoon

RELATED TO: Raccoons are distantly related to weasels and skunks and are more closely related to coatis and kinkajous of Central and South America.

SIZE: Up to 3 feet (1 m) long from the nose to the tip of the tail, and about 13 to 15 pounds (about 6 to 7 kg)

NATIVE TO NORTH AMERICA: Yes. Raccoons are found throughout the lower forty-eight states of the United States. Their range extends up into southern Canada and down as far as Panama in Central America.

ENDANGERED: No (Raccoons are listed by the International Union for the Conservation of Nature as a Species of Least Concern.)

It turns out that we humans have provided excellent substitutes for both kinds of natural den sites. Attic crawl spaces and gaps under the eaves of a roof or under a deck or a porch make excellent burrows. A chimney is just about the same diameter as the hollow trees the raccoons favor in more natural settings.

MEASURING SUCCESS

Once it's moved into human space, why is the raccoon so successful? Biologists point to several traits. The first is body size. Raccoons are mesocarnivores, which means they are medium-sized (*meso*) mammals that get up to three-quarters of their diet as meat. (That's where *carnivore* comes

in.) We humans offer a nonstop banquet of meat-based pet food, kitchen garbage, and remnants of takeout. Researcher Stanley Gehrt of Ohio State University has even seen fights break out among urban raccoons over french fries and doughnuts.

The second trait underlying the raccoon's success is its ability to climb. Raccoons have the claws, flexible spine, and agility required to scale trees and buildings. This allows them to escape predators, exploit new food sources, and take advantage of more and better den sites.

The third trait is the animal's dexterity—the raccoon's ability to manipulate objects with its handlike paws. The whole paw of the raccoon appears to work as a sensory organ. Whiskers on the paws help the animal identify objects by feel.

LIKE HUMANS, RACCOONS HAVE FIVE DIGITS ON EACH PAW. ALTHOUGH THEY CANNOT STRETCH THUMB TO LITTLE FINGER, THEIR FINGERS ARE EXTREMELY NIMBLE. THEY CAN GRASP JUST ABOUT ANYTHING, TURN DOORKNOBS—AND CLIMB INTO GARBAGE CANS, NO PROBLEM!

Biologist Andrew Iwaniuk conducted a study of dexterity in carnivores, ranking them on a scale of 1 to 21. Hyenas ranked near the bottom, raccoons near the top.

Finally, raccoons are really smart. Raccoons in the wild and in captivity share two traits linked to intelligence: they are curious and they are playful. They explore their surroundings and often play with objects they find. Gordon Burghardt of the University of Kentucky thinks that playfulness in species such as raccoons and cebus monkeys may have grown out of these animals' need to search and probe among leaf litter, under rocks, and inside hollow logs. The skills they use in foraging—including handling objects, recognizing edible foods, and learning what's tasty and how to get it—seem to translate into treating objects as toys, Burghardt says.

Handy, smart, playful, curious. That sounds a lot like us. Is it any wonder raccoons flourish alongside humans in our cities and suburbs?

ARE WE CREATING SUPER RACCOONS?

Urban raccoons live different lives than their wild cousins. For example, raccoons born in the city remain with their mothers longer than raccoons born in the wild. They spend a full year learning the ways of city life, what the best den sites are, and where to find them before setting off on their own.

FROM RASCAL TO *RASUKARU*

After the publication of *Rascal,* Sterling North's 1963 children's book about life with his pet raccoon, children the world over dreamed of having their own masked Rascal. *Rascal* was made into a movie by Walt Disney in 1969. Later, the story was made into an anime series, *Araiguma rasukaru* (Rascal the raccoon), that aired in Japan in 1977. The series was so popular that Japanese families wanted to have raccoons for pets. Japan imported about eighteen hundred raccoons to meet the demand. Some of the animals escaped and bred. As a result, this iconic North American mammal is found throughout Japan, where it competes for space and food with the tanuki, or raccoon dog, a raccoon species native to Japan.

But that may not be the most significant way in which city life is changing raccoons. Suzanne E. MacDonald, a psychologist at York University in Toronto, Canada, believes humans may be inadvertently creating a race of super raccoons. As we try to control the animals, we are providing them with harder and harder puzzles. For example, to keep them out of our trash, we have raccoon-proof trash barrels. Only the smartest raccoons figure out how to get into these barrels. This ends up ensuring that only the smartest animals thrive and pass on their genes to the next generation of raccoons.

CHAPTER 2

THE LION IN THE HEADLIGHTS

LOS ANGELES, CALIFORNIA

YOU MIGHT THINK THAT THE ONLY LIONS IN SOUTHERN CALIFORNIA ARE IN SAN DIEGO'S ZOO. BUT IN MAY 2012, THE CITY OF SANTA MONICA SENT OUT AN E-MAIL ALERTING RESIDENTS TO A SIGHTING. A lion had been spotted downtown, just blocks from a farmers' market and a preschool. The e-mail said the following:

> **2nd St. between Wilshire and Arizona is closed down to vehicular and pedestrian traffic due to a mountain lion sighting. The lion is contained and the Department of Fish and Game is en route.**

The lion was a young male looking for territory to call his own. Biologists think he had wandered into the outskirts of the city during the night, only to find himself in the busy downtown area when the sun came up.

CYCLISTS AND PEDESTRIANS CROWD DOWNTOWN SANTA MONICA, CALIFORNIA, NOT FAR FROM WHERE A MOUNTAIN LION FOUND HIS WAY IN THE SPRING OF 2012.

The *Los Angeles Times* reported that the animal wandered down Arizona Avenue before entering an office courtyard and surprising a janitor, who called police. The police fired pepper-spray pellets and water from a fire hose to contain the lion.

MOUNTAIN LIONS ARE SOLITARY ANIMALS THAT WILL AVOID CONFRONTATION WHENEVER POSSIBLE. IF FRIGHTENED, THE ANIMAL MAY DISPLAY AGGRESSIVE BEHAVIOR, SUCH AS FLATTENING THE EARS AND DISPLAYING ITS TEETH.

MOUNTAIN LION FACTS

The mountain lion is North America's largest cat. It is a solitary hunter, stalking and ambushing its favorite prey, deer. When deer aren't on the menu, mountain lions have been known to eat wild pigs, raccoons, and even armadillos.

SCIENTIFIC NAME: *Puma concolor*

ALSO KNOWN AS: cougar, puma, catamount

RELATED TO: The mountain lion shares the genus *Puma* with the jaguarundi. The mountain lion is more distantly related to other big cats, including lions, tigers, cheetahs, and jaguars.

SIZE: Males are 40 to 60 inches (1 to 1.5 m) long, not including the tail, and weigh from 80 to 265 pounds (36 to 120 kg). Females are 34 to 52 inches (0.9 to 1.3 m) long and weigh from 64 to 171 pounds (29 to 78 kg).

NATIVE TO NORTH AMERICA: Yes. The range of this widespread species extends from Canada south to the tip of South America.

ENDANGERED: No (The mountain lion is listed by the International Union for the Conservation of Nature as a Species of Least Concern. Its status may decline, however, as the species loses habitat and genetic diversity.)

Then they shot the lion with a dart gun, hoping to knock it out. Before the drug could take effect, the frightened animal tried to escape into the street. For the safety of people nearby, the lion was shot and killed.

DOWN FROM THE HILLS, ONTO THE HIGHWAYS

Mountain lions do their best to avoid people and stay out of sight. In the wild, they slip through the woods and mountains, making very little noise. They prefer habitat that provides plenty of white-tailed deer for food. They also like wooded areas and other cover from which they can stalk and pounce on their prey. Most of the time, mountain lions pounce on deer. Only rarely do they pounce on a hiker or a mountain biker who has come into the animal's territory.

It's no surprise that people are sighting lions in the backyards of Los Angeles's exclusive hillside neighborhoods. People there have built homes right up to the edge of the wilderness where mountain lions live. Landscaping around the homes provides lots of tasty plants for deer to browse. Where the deer go, lions follow. Pet food left outside can attract raccoons that in turn attract lions. Dogs chained in a yard can look like a tasty snack to a hungry lion.

Once lions venture into human cities such as Los Angeles, they face tremendous dangers from the highways that connect neighborhoods. They are struck by cars and killed. The habitat they need to hunt and raise families is replaced by wide bands of highway asphalt. Highways open up wilderness to more development—and more loss of habitat. But perhaps the greatest harm highways pose to lions is that these roads create barriers. They prevent lions from moving freely within a large territory. As a result of the roads, the lion territory is carved into smaller and smaller pieces. Biologists call this carving up of the landscape habitat fragmentation.

As habitat is fragmented, the lions' lives are disrupted. They may not be able to safely cross busy highways as they pursue deer. With less territory to wander, they may have fewer mates—or none at all. And young males that need to establish their own territories find themselves trapped in the home ranges of older males. Often young males stranded on habitat islands are killed by older males in fights over territory.

ON THE TRACK OF LIONS

Seth Riley and Jeff Sikich are biologists with the National Park Service. Since 2002 they have been studying the mountain lions that live in the mountains of Ventura and Los Angeles counties in Southern California. The biologists want to know how urban development is affecting the lions.

Since 2002 Riley and Sikich have collared and tagged twenty-six mountain lions. They put collars equipped with GPS (global positioning system) loggers onto the animals.

RESEARCHERS WITH THE UNIVERSITY OF CALIFORNIA–DAVIS EXAMINE A COLLARED MOUNTAIN LION. AS LIONS AND HUMANS COME INTO MORE FREQUENT CONTACT IN URBAN AREAS, RESEARCHERS ARE WORKING TO LEARN MORE ABOUT THE ANIMALS' BEHAVIOR TO BETTER PROTECT BOTH HUMANS AND LIONS.

LEARNING TO WALK ON THE WILD SIDE

Students at De Anza College near San Jose in Northern California are training to become wildlife corridor technicians. These technicians will work to help the animals that use wildlife corridors such as the lion tunnel. Their classroom is San Jose's Coyote Valley, an important stop for migrating birds. The valley is also home to elk, bobcat, coyote, and mountain lions. Students in the college's environmental studies program earn a certificate as wildlife corridor technicians by learning to identify native species, observe them in the wild, track them, and identify their signs. They then use those skills to help plan, construct, and maintain places for wildlife to move through the Coyote Valley.

AN INSTRUCTOR WITH DE ANZA COLLEGE'S WILDLIFE CORRIDOR TECHNICIAN PROGRAM SEARCHES THE DRY BED OF A CREEK RUNNING THROUGH SAN JOSE'S COYOTE VALLEY. SHE IS LOOKING FOR SIGNS OF ANIMALS. NOTICE THE RACCOON PRINTS IN THE BOTTOM LEFT CORNER OF THE PHOTO.

For Ryan Bourbour, studying to be a wildlife corridor technician meant learning to "read" roadkill. Every day he and the other students in the De Anza College van would see deer, coyotes, and other animals that had been struck and killed. To Bourbour each dead animal "meant there was something wrong with the way we build our roads, something we need to fix."

Wildlife corridor technicians learn to identify species by sight and by their signs (tracks and scat, or droppings). They learn how to place and angle a camera trap (a motion-activated trail camera) for filming animal movements. This helps the technicians identify choke points, places where wildlife tend to move across highways. Students are also trained in interpreting GPS data and reading topographical maps. These maps show hills, valleys, and other features of the landscape.

A typical day in the field means bushwhacking through rough terrain, crawling through culverts (drainpipes) choked with spiderwebs, and dodging trucks on highways. It's exhausting, and students often go home covered in poison oak or ticks. But it's exhilarating too.

Fellow student Breanna Martinico says about her efforts, "A wildlife corridor technician works with city officials to inform them and encourage them to keep critical areas open. We try to show them the ways that open space benefits the community more than money that would be brought in from a new shopping center. My ultimate goal as a wildlife corridor technician is to protect the right of species to move across the land, which means identifying key areas and also working to get them permanently protected."

After his first class, Bourbour, a city kid, felt he was seeing his environment for the first time. And he was motivated to protect it. "Without wildlife corridors, biodiversity will continue to decline. One reality we connect with in the program is that establishing and maintaining wildlife corridors isn't just critical for wildlife, it's critical for the future of people, too."

At regular intervals, the GPS logger beams the lions' location to a satellite, which bounces the information to a data collection center the scientists can then access. The data from the collars helps them get a picture of the lions' movements. How easily are the lions moving around their territory? Are they mating and raising families?

The GPS collar data revealed a small and shrinking population of lions hemmed in by highways. The two counties have two main lion populations. One is in the Los Padres National Forest. The other is to the south in the Santa Monica Mountains. Lions in search of deer, mates, or territory have to cross three highway barriers on their way between Los Padres and the mountains.

At first, the scientists doubted any lion could make it across those barriers. But a male named P12 (*P* for "puma," a mountain lion) proved them wrong. In December 2008, Sikich first captured and collared P12 in the Simi Hills north of Route 101. He was recaptured to the south in the Santa Monica Mountains a few months later. To get there, P12 had to cross all three highway barriers. Using GPS collar data and DNA samples from other lions, Riley and Sikich learned that P12 had mated with a female, P13, from the Santa Monica Mountains.

NEW GENES, NEW HOPE

The mountain lion's future depends on genetic diversity. As lion populations are hemmed in by highways, they can become inbred. When closely

HIGHWAYS IN LOS ANGELES OFTEN CUT THROUGH THE TERRITORIAL RANGE OF MOUNTAIN LIONS AND OTHER WILD ANIMALS. WITH OBSTRUCTIONS SUCH AS THESE, THE ANIMALS HAVE DIFFICULTY CROSSING FROM ONE PART OF THEIR RANGE TO ANOTHER IN SEARCH OF FOOD AND MATES.

related lions mate, their offspring lack the mix of genes to keep them healthy. The biologists knew from a DNA test that P13 was herself the offspring of a father-daughter inbreeding. When she and P12 mated, he was contributing much-needed genetic diversity.

Of the three kittens P12 sired, only a female, P19, survived to breed. P19 had her first litter in 2012. Each of P19's kittens carried some of the new genes from the population of lions in Los Padres National Forest.

WILDLIFE OVERPASSES, SUCH AS THIS ONE IN MONTANA, ARE A CREATIVE SOLUTION TO ALLOW WILD ANIMALS TO MOVE SAFELY ACROSS HIGHWAYS.

Xʷíxʷeyúɫ Nxɫews
ANIMALS' BRIDGE

FINDING SOLUTIONS

The best solution to protecting genetic diversity is to make sure the Los Angeles lions can move easily across their range. The National Park Service biologists are working with California's Department of Transportation to create a way for lions to cross one of the busy highways that divides the lions' habitat. They know from collar data where most lions come right up to the freeway and turn around. Biologists and highway officials plan to create a 13-by-13-foot (4 by 4 m) tunnel at that spot to allow lions and other wildlife to go under the highway. Fences along the freeway will help funnel animals to the tunnel. Once the tunnel is in place, it should allow lions and fresh genes to move freely—and safely—between the two lion populations of Los Angeles.

Will California have room for lions and people in the future? The lions are facing tough odds, and no one has a crystal ball. But one thing is certain. The lions will only survive if Californians decide they want to live in a state that still makes room for wild things—even wild things with sharp teeth.

CHAPTER 3

THE CROW IN THE CROSSWALK

TOKYO, JAPAN

TOKYO IS HOME TO TENS OF THOUSANDS OF URBAN CROWS. THE RELATIONSHIP BETWEEN THE CITY'S HUMAN RESIDENTS AND ITS CROWS IS ANYTHING BUT PEACEFUL. In 2001 one of the large, black birds dive-bombed a golfer on one of the city's many golf courses. That golfer just happened to be Shintaro Ishihara, Tokyo's governor (like a mayor in North America). Not amused, Ishihara famously vowed to make "crow meat pie" into Japan's national dish.

Ishihara had declared war on a crafty adversary. The crows in Tokyo are jungle crows. These relatives of the common North American species of crow have larger bodies and beaks. All crows are smart. And jungle crows are one of the best of these brainy birds in coming up with clever ways to make use of new sources of food.

In Tokyo these smart birds have learned to scavenge from household trash cans, from picnic tables, and from parks where people feed ducks and fish. The boldest crows will even snatch food directly from the stalls of snack vendors in a city park.

> URBAN JUNGLE CROWS ARE OPPORTUNISTS. THEY SCAVENGE FOR FOOD, AND HUMANS MAKE IT EASY WHEN THEY DO NOT CAREFULLY DISPOSE OF BAG LUNCHES AND OTHER FOOD WASTE.

JUNGLE CROWS EAT JUST ABOUT ANYTHING. THEY CAN MAKE A MEAL OF SEEDS, FRUIT, SMALL ANIMALS, OR FOOD SCRAPS FROM HUMAN GARBAGE. THE ANIMAL'S SCIENTIFIC NAME (*CORVUS MACRORHYNCHOS*) MEANS "LARGE-BEAKED CROW."

JUNGLE CROW FACTS

SCIENTIFIC NAME: *Corvus macrorhynchos*

This crow has a heavy, arched bill. It looks more like a raven than the common crow in North America. It is found from Afghanistan across Asia to the Philippines.

ALSO KNOWN AS: Large-billed crow

RELATED TO: Crows, ravens, and jays

SIZE: They are about 18 to 23 inches (46 to 58 centimeters) long.

NATIVE TO JAPAN: Yes

ENDANGERED: No (The jungle crow is listed by the International Union for the Conservation of Nature as a Species of Least Concern.)

BAGS OF GARBAGE ON THE STREETS OF TOKYO ATTRACT URBAN CROWS. TOKYO IS A DENSELY POPULATED CITY WHERE BIRDS AND HUMANS COMPETE FOR SPACE AND OTHER RESOURCES.

IT ALL BEGAN WITH GARBAGE

Where did the crows come from? The answer goes back to a change the city made in the way it collected garbage.

Before 1986 fewer Japanese women worked outside the home. They were home during the day to put away the garbage cans after trash collection. In the late 1980s, Japanese women began to enter the workforce in larger numbers. Suddenly no one was home to put away the trash cans. So large numbers of trash cans were left on the street during the day, causing traffic jams. To solve the problem, city leaders had residents switch from trash cans to dark-colored garbage bags. In 1993 the city began a recycling program. Clear, see-through bags replaced the dark bags so garbage collectors could see the paper, glass, and plastic contents inside.

The rise in the population of crows started

around 1986. Plastic garbage bags were easy for the birds to pierce with their beaks. The crow population rose again in the mid-1990s, likely because the clear bags allowed them to see and zero in on the best food scraps.

But the crows' nesting behavior created a more serious problem than raiding garbage. And this problem also arose from an everyday behavior of Tokyo's human citizens that just happened to fit in with something the crows do naturally. In this case, it wasn't putting out the garbage. It was doing the laundry.

A MESSY NEST PROBLEM

Tokyo is one of the most densely settled cities on the planet, and space is tight. Apartments are small, and many do not have clothes dryers. For this reason, residents use wire coat hangers to hang their wet clothing outside the window on balconies.

Jungle crows like to build their large, messy nests from sturdy twigs. And what could be sturdier than a wire coat hanger? Tokyo's jungle crows quickly adapted to using wire—and even

CROWS VS. THE BULLET TRAIN

Japan is an island nation. Its two biggest islands, Honshu and Kyushu, are linked by high-speed electric trains (*below*). Because of their speed and streamlined shape, they are known as bullet trains, or *shinkansen*. The shinkansen can reach speeds of almost 190 miles (300 kilometers) per hour. Each year, 150 million people ride Japan's bullet trains.

The lowly jungle crow brought this technological marvel to a halt in 2007. That year, crows nesting on a power station caused a blackout in the Japanese prefecture (state) of Akita on the island of Honshu. The power outage briefly stopped the mighty bullet train in its tracks.

fiber-optic cable—as well as twigs in their nests. The crows liked to build their nests on top of utility poles. But this was a problem for humans. A single stray wire from a crow's nest could make

TOKYO CROWS LIKE TO BUILD NESTS ON UTILITY POLES. AS UTILITY WORKERS BEGAN TO DESTROY THE NESTS, THE CROWS GOT SMART. THEY BUILT FAKE NESTS!

contact with a power line, disrupting electricity and blacking out entire sections of the city. When the blackouts caused by crows' nests began to affect half a million people, the power company in Tokyo had to do something.

SEND OUT THE CROW PATROL

Utility companies in Japan set up crow patrols. These utility workers in Tokyo and other large metropolitan areas in Japan scour the city looking for crow's nests on power poles. When they find them, they remove the nests. But the crows began to build decoy nests. In addition to the crow patrol, Tokyo residents cover their garbage with crow-proof netting and place garbage in yellow bags (crows supposedly can't see through yellow). The city has started collecting garbage in the middle of the night before the birds get a chance to scavenge. To control the number of crows, the city also traps them and kills them. But

URBAN CROWS ARE A NUISANCE IN MANY PARTS OF JAPAN. THIS MEMBER OF A CROW PATROL IN KAGOSHIMA, ON JAPAN'S KYUSHU ISLAND, IS SCOUTING FOR NESTS ON UTILITY POLES.

it's expensive to kill the birds, about fifty dollars per crow. Over the last ten years, Tokyo has spent millions to combat its crow problem. And just as fast as the city kills the crows, more birds fly in from the suburbs to replace them. The crow population is on the rise.

LIVING ON THE EDGE

Some animals—like Tokyo's crows—do really well in the suburbs and in the city. Ecologists call these animals habitat generalists, meaning they can be more flexible than other species about where they live. As long as they can find food, shelter, and a mate, these animals are happy with what the city and the suburbs have to offer.

Some of these species do especially well on the edge of cities. Ecologists call these animals edge species. They can be found where one habitat meets another, such as where the woods meet a lawn. Many familiar backyard birds— mockingbirds, house wrens, and song sparrows—

BRAINY BIRDS

Birds that do well in the city have to figure out how to navigate in a world of steel, glass, and concrete. They have to adjust to noise from traffic and machinery such as leaf blowers and air conditioners. And if they are to thrive and become true city dwellers, they have to master some of our human technology. Are birds up to the task?

It seems they are. Researchers have reported sparrows that have learned to trigger the electronic beam that opens automatic doors to get to the food crumbs at a railroad station café in Hamilton, New Zealand. Swallows have learned a similar trick to open a lumberyard entryway at a Home Depot in Maplewood, Minnesota. The birds swoop in front of the motion detector that operates the automatic double doors. They then nest inside the lumberyard, safe from predators. Scientists think that birds may even be changing their songs to be better heard in the city environment.

are edge species. Many of these birds are omnivores, eating a wide range of plant foods as well as worms and insects. They also tend to stay put. Instead of migrating in the fall, they hang around the whole year, rounding out their diets with the seed and suet from our bird feeders.

When human cities and roadways break up natural habitat into smaller and smaller pieces, two things happen to the birds that live there. The first is that the number of species goes down. Small habitat fragments aren't able to support the same variety of species as larger areas of habitat.

The second thing that happens is that the mix of bird species changes. Specialists—birds that are fussy about the place they call home—are forced out. Replacing them are habitat generalists and edge species—like crows.

BECOMING URBAN

Urban animals change their behavior profoundly to fit into city life. They are willing to live packed tightly together, in smaller territories—just like humans in an apartment building. They may stay in the city all year-round, giving up their seasonal migration. The milder, steadier climate of some cities also creates ideal conditions for raising a family. Species can mate and bear young throughout the year instead of only seasonally.

Scientists call this ability to change behavior plasticity. The behavior of these species is easily shaped, just like plastic. They are able to make their homes in a wide variety of habitats. They eat a broad range of foods, some provided by humans in the form of trash or handouts. They will nest or make their dens in a variety of man-made structures. Over time, they also become much less afraid of people. Some even become tame. Scientists refer to this trend as "reducing the

escape distance"—the distance an animal likes to keep between itself and a potential predator, such as humans.

Can the people of Tokyo find a way to outsmart the crafty crows? One surprising solution may be honeybees. Since 2005 the Ginza Honey Bee Project has been encouraging Tokyo residents, from architects to schoolkids to homemakers, to become urban beekeepers. Twenty-four office buildings and one department store now have hives on their rooftops. The hives produce honey and another benefit—tiny, winged crow patrols. It turns out that honeybees will attack crows and drive them away. But with nearly twenty-two thousand crows calling Tokyo home, it will take a lot of bees to solve the crow problem.

CHAPTER 4
THE COYOTE IN THE SUB SHOP

CHICAGO, ILLINOIS

ONE APRIL MORNING IN 2007, THE EMPLOYEES AND CUSTOMERS IN A CHICAGO QUIZNOS SUBMARINE SANDWICH SHOP WERE STARTLED TO SEE A COYOTE STROLL THROUGH THE OPEN DOOR. Finding himself surrounded by people, the coyote panicked and tried to leap back over the counter. He landed in the beverage cooler instead. There he remained, while customers snapped his picture with their phones. The episode made the national news, and people worldwide were captivated by a viral video of the coyote posing among the bottles of neon-colored juice drinks.

Animal control officers captured the coyote and took him to an animal shelter where Chicago's Animal Care and Control staff checked his health. They named him Adrian, after the animal control employee who watched him overnight. The Quiznos employees visited the coyote and brought him a prime-rib sandwich as an offering of friendship. But the animal control veterinarian wouldn't allow Adrian to eat the sub. There are no sub shops in the wild, and that was where Adrian was going to be released.

The coyote was transferred to a wildlife rehabilitation center. On April 5, 2007, employees of Flint Creek Wildlife Rehabilitation placed Adrian in a dog carrier and drove him to private land outside the city. The owner of the land was happy to have another coyote on her property. As reporters looked on, the Flint Creek staff removed the top of the carrier, and Adrian leaped out and ran for the woods.

Adrian was not the only coyote to wander into downtown Chicago that year. An additional ten to fifteen coyotes were trapped within the city limits in 2007. A few years later, in February 2012, a coyote led police on a chase through Chicago's South Side.

ADRIAN THE COYOTE GOT TRAPPED IN THE COOLER AT A QUIZNOS SHOP IN CHICAGO IN 2007. OF THE HUNDREDS OF URBAN NUISANCE COYOTES IN ILLINOIS EACH YEAR, MORE THAN HALF ARE IN THE CHICAGO AREA.

COYOTE FACTS

The ancestor of the coyote prowled North America during the last ice age about 1.8 million years ago. A grassland predator, coyotes thrived as humans cleared forests for farmland over the last two centuries. The animal continued to adapt as cities replaced farms. The coyote is found in every U.S. state except Hawaii.

SCIENTIFIC NAME: *Canis latrans*

ALSO KNOWN AS: Prairie wolf, American jackal

RELATED TO: Other canids, including wolves and domestic dogs

SIZE: 2.5 to 3 feet (0.8 to 0.9 m) long and up to 45 pounds (20 kg)

NATIVE TO NORTH AMERICA: Yes

ENDANGERED: No (The coyote is listed by the International Union for the Conservation of Nature as a Species of Least Concern.)

A TRICKSTER IN ANY LANGUAGE

Canids (coyotes, foxes, and other doglike mammals in the family Canidae) appear in folklore and legends around the world. They are typically clever tricksters—heroes who break social rules and conventions. Here are some common mythic canid characters:

NORTH AMERICA: Coyote is a trickster in Native American storytelling traditions from California to the Great Plains. Farther east, Tsu-la the fox plays a trick on a rabbit in a Cherokee folktale. African Americans in the South told tales of a trickster known as Brer Fox.

AFRICA AND THE CARIBBEAN: Anansi the Spider can turn himself into a fox.

EUROPE: Reynard the Fox appears in folktales from France that date to the 1100s.

ASIA: In Japanese folklore, the fox, or *kitsune*, has supernatural powers. In India and Nepal, the golden jackal (related to coyotes) takes on the role of trickster.

AUSTRALIA: The devil dog appears in the legends of the Lardil people of Australia's Northern Territory.

AMERICAN CARTOONIST CHUCK JONES CREATED THE WILE E. COYOTE "SUPER GENIUS" CHARACTER IN THE LATE 1940S. THE CRAFTY COYOTE IS KNOWN FOR HIS CRAZY SCHEMES.

TRICKSTERS

Coyotes were in North America long before the first people arrived. The coyote has long been a symbol of the American West and the hero of Native American stories and legends. For the last century, the animal has been steadily expanding its range eastward. As people left the countryside to live in suburbs and cities, these furry tricksters with their sharp teeth followed. Coyotes are now found from coast to coast.

THE COYOTE PROJECT

One of the cities in North America where the coyote has flourished is Chicago, Illinois.

In the 1990s, coyotes began to move into the Chicago metropolitan area in greater numbers. No one is really sure why; perhaps because people were hunting fewer coyotes. In earlier years, fewer than 20 coyotes would be trapped and removed from the city limits in a given year. But by the end of the twentieth century, up to 350 were being trapped each year.

Coyotes are the largest carnivore found in most North American cities. Yet wildlife biologists knew very little about these urban coyotes. How were their lives different from the lives of coyotes in the grasslands of the American West? What did urban coyotes eat, whom did they socialize with, how did they move around the city, and how did they manage to survive in the urban setting? Did they pose a risk to people? In 2000 Ohio State University biologist Stanley Gehrt set out to find the answers to these questions.

Gehrt and his colleagues set up the Coyote Project, the first study of Chicago's urban coyotes. It focused on Cook County, the county in which Chicago lies. The area is home to more than 5 million people. The project team trapped coyotes and fitted them with radio (VHF) or GPS collars and identifying ear tags. In about twelve years, they collared almost four hundred urban coyotes.

The collars allowed the researchers to track the coyotes any time of day or night. On maps of the city, the location of each coyote shows up as a colored dot. As the years passed, thirty thousand of these dots began to form a picture of the animals' lives.

Over the years, Gehrt and his colleagues have captured and collared coyotes from many different packs. One pack was headed by a female they dubbed Big Mama and her mate, Coyote #115. Their territory included Chicago's O'Hare Airport,

one of the nation's busiest airports. Another pack included Coyote #441, whose territory included Chicago's Lincoln Park Zoo and one of its busiest downtown roadways, Lake Shore Drive. A third was the pack that included Coyote #434.

THE STORY OF COYOTE #434

Coyote #434 was a ten-month-old female. She was first captured in February 2010 in a marshy area surrounded by dense human development. At the time of her capture, #434 was part of a pack that moved within a 180-acre (73-hectare) territory that included the village of Schaumburg, Illinois, a suburb of Chicago. Researchers fitted her with a GPS collar and released her where she was found. Signals from the device bounced her location off a satellite to the researchers' computer every ten minutes, giving them a detailed picture of her movements.

At first, #434 remained with her pack near the marsh and the surrounding woods. When she moved around her territory, she followed the area's power lines, avoiding houses and people. She also avoided yards and parks, even those without fences or other barriers to keep her out. By the end of that summer, she was full grown and beginning to separate from her pack. Throughout the fall, she was solitary, moving over a large area that includes Chicago and a dozen surrounding counties.

But by November 2010, she had come to the

A COYOTE SURVEYS HIS TERRAIN. COYOTES ARE PACK ANIMALS, THOUGH THEY WILL SOMETIMES HUNT SOLO.

attention of the Department of Natural Resources as a nuisance coyote—one that has lost its shyness around people and that poses a potential risk to people and pets. Ruth McIntyre lived in a northwestern suburb of Chicago. She had called the department complaining that a coyote was stalking squirrels in her backyard. McIntyre's neighbor was putting out food for deer and squirrels, and McIntyre herself had been putting out food for the neighborhood's many stray cats. Such easy pickings were too much for Coyote #434 to resist.

At about this same time, the coyote's GPS collar fell off. (The collars are programmed to fall off so the animal doesn't have to wear it forever.) Gehrt and his colleagues were no longer able to track her. Nonetheless, she does still carry an ear tag, so if she were to visit the McIntyre backyard again, she would be easy to identify. For now, her fate is unknown.

COYOTE LESSONS

Researchers know that Coyote #434 is typical of urban coyotes. If humans put out food that attracts wildlife—as did McIntyre and her neighbors—coyotes will learn to visit a backyard for an easy handout. From the twelve-year study, researchers also learned that coyotes prey on common suburban animals such as white-tailed deer and Canada geese. This helps keep those populations from growing too big. In general, however, coyotes will stick to their natural diet of rodents, rabbits, and fruit.

The study also shows that urban coyotes pose very little risk to humans as disease carriers. In fact, urban coyotes appear to lead healthier, longer lives than coyotes in rural areas. Some of the urban coyotes from the study had heartworms, which didn't harm them and can't be passed along to people. About one in ten coyotes suffered from the skin disease mange—no matter where the coyote lived. Mange can kill a coyote, but it doesn't make them aggressive toward people. Most of the coyotes captured in the Coyote Project were in "great physical condition," Gehrt says.

The study also showed that coyotes do their best to avoid contact with people. Problems with coyotes tend to happen when humans deliberately feed or attract wildlife, creating a source of prey close to where people live and work.

"Programs to control coyotes need to target nuisance coyotes, instead of targeting the whole coyote population," Gehrt explains. "If we trap and remove or even kill coyotes, they are quickly replaced. In order to manage coyotes, we have to manage ourselves."

That means education. Through informative talks at libraries and through outreach programs at schools, parks, and nature centers, the researchers from the Coyote Project are teaching Chicagoans about coyotes. By knowing more about the animals' natural behavior and how to adapt ourselves to it, the programs are helping ensure peaceful coexistence with this cunning trickster who has long captivated our imaginations.

CHAPTER 5

THE FLYING FOXES IN THE PARK

SYDNEY, AUSTRALIA

WHAT IF THOUSANDS OF BATS DECIDED TO MOVE INTO YOUR BACKYARD? NOT JUST ANY BATS BUT MEGABATS, FLYING FOXES WITH A 3-FOOT (1 M) WINGSPAN. For the city of Sydney, Australia, it wasn't a "what if" question. By 2010 the bat situation had gotten pretty desperate.

For one thing, it was a very special backyard. Flying foxes had taken a liking to the Royal Botanic Gardens on Sydney's harbor. Founded in 1816, the garden has 74 acres (30 hectares) of plants and trees from Australia and around the world. Since the 1890s, a small colony of flying foxes had called the Royal Botanic Gardens home. But by the 1990s, their numbers had climbed to thirty thousand.

They were gray-headed flying foxes, to be exact. Hanging upside down from tree branches, with their wings wrapped tightly around their bodies, these megabats look like little Draculas in leathery capes. But unlike Dracula, flying foxes live on nectar and fruit, not blood.

WHY ARE FLYING FOXES IN SYDNEY?

As Australians have cleared the continent's forests to make way for farms and fruit orchards, flying foxes have moved ever closer to the cities. City life can be pretty attractive if you are a flying fox. Living close to human houses, shops, and offices, flying foxes are safe from the guns of human hunters. Well-watered trees in suburbs and cities have plenty of leaves, providing a reliable source of fruit and pollen. Trees in the wild, on the other hand, often lose their leaves during frequent dry spells and don't bear as much fruit. Experts think that city streetlights may make it easier for flying foxes to make their way to leafy trees.

GRAY-HEADED FLYING FOXES HAVE AN IMPRESSIVE WINGSPAN AND ARE VERY GRACEFUL FLYERS.

GRAY-HEADED FLYING FOX FACTS

Flying foxes aren't related to foxes at all. They belong to a family of large fruit-eating bats called megabats. The gray-headed flying fox is the largest bat in Australia. Other bats use echolocation (using supersonic chirps as radar) to find and target the insects they eat. Flying

SCIENTIFIC NAME: *Pteropus poliocephalus*

ALSO KNOWN AS: Fruit bat

RELATED TO: There are 185 other species of fruit bats found in Africa, the Middle East, India, Southeast Asia, and northern

SIZE: The average weight is about 1.5 pounds (0.7 kg). The wingspan is up to 3 feet (1 m).

NATIVE TO AUSTRALIA: Yes

ENDANGERED: Flying foxes are considered

DO FLYING FOXES MAKE GOOD NEIGHBORS?

In the Sydney suburb of Gordon, the Ku-ring-gai Flying-fox Reserve has a resident colony of forty thousand flying foxes. During the height of the Australian summer, that number can nearly double to seventy thousand. The reserve is surrounded by Gordon's human population of six thousand. Some of Gordon's residents object to the squawking and musky smell and purple bat poop on walkways, cars, and playgrounds. They also worry that bats can spread disease. Flying foxes do carry two diseases: Australian bat lyssavirus, which resembles rabies, and hendra virus, a disease that can pass from bats to humans by way of horses. However, scientists think that hendra virus may only spread to other species by way of a different species of flying fox. Some residents of Gordon want the government to remove the bats that are already in the reserve. But there is nowhere for the bats to go.

Other people, such as members of the Ku-ring-gai Bat Conservation Society, argue that efforts to move the bats will stress them and force them into less suitable habitat. Bat advocates argue for establishing buffer zones around existing camps and restoring bat habitat to increase places for bats to roost farther away from heavily populated areas.

seeds, making them an essential part of a healthy forest community. However, climate change is altering and shortening the times that native trees flower. As a result, the trees bear less fruit and less food is available to flying foxes in the Australian bush, or wilderness. And during extended heat waves in the bush—related to global warming—heat stress can make the animals sick or kill them outright. "We don't think of a city as being a wildlife refuge, but then again we don't perceive Sydney the way a flying fox does," Eby says. The city has fig, eucalyptus, ironbark, and other native trees that provide flying foxes with shelter and food. And the city provides protection from the effects of climate change, especially drought.

Eby predicts that flying foxes will continue to move into Australia's cities. "That presents us with challenges that we are ill-prepared to meet. We need to reconsider Sydney as not just a human space but a space we share with wildlife, flying foxes, and other species. We need to be

But the main reason flying foxes are in Australia's cities is that there are few other wild places for them to go. Bat ecologist Peggy Eby explains that flying foxes spread pollen and carry

FLYING FOXES LIVE IN LARGE COLONIES OF UP TO ONE MILLION BATS. WITH FEWER PLACES TO ROOST, THE SIZE OF THE COLONIES KEEPS GROWING. THOUSANDS OF BATS IN SYDNEY'S ROYAL BOTANIC GARDENS HAVE STRIPPED TREES THERE OF LEAVES AND BARK.

imaginative and creative and come up with some pragmatic ways to accommodate wildlife in what we have considered to be our space."

SETTING UP CAMP IN SYDNEY

The colony of flying foxes in Sydney set up camp in a grove of rare palms and other native Australian trees in the botanic gardens. These palms are some of the oldest trees in the gardens' collection. Because the grove has more than two hundred species of wild and cultivated palm trees, it is a living museum of rare plants. Botanists study these trees as an important part of the efforts to save them.

Flying foxes don't build nests, but they do live together in camps, gathering in trees to roost (hang from branches) and rest. The problem is that a roosting colony of thousands of flying foxes weighs a lot. The combined weight can snap off branches, and as the flying foxes move around, they can break off leaves and bark. In the wild, flying foxes shift from tree to tree. This allows the tree leaves to grow back. But when their territory is fragmented, the animals roost in whatever is left of their home forest. They stay put, and that's when the damage to trees begins.

Back in the 1890s, the director of the botanic gardens called in the local rifle club to shoot the flying foxes. But shooting the animals is no longer an option for controlling their numbers. Gray-headed flying foxes are an endangered species. So instead, the garden staff set up bright strobe lights in the trees to discourage the flying foxes from nesting there. Staff even hung bags of python poop in the trees as a flying-fox repellent. Nothing worked.

LOUD ENOUGH FOR YOU?

So the botanic gardens worked with Australia's Department of Sustainability and the Environment on a plan to drive out the flying foxes by blasting loud industrial noise at them from speakers mounted on golf carts. The hope was that the colony would merge with another colony of flying foxes roosting in a nature reserve in the nearby suburb of Gordon. The noise solution had been used successfully with a colony of flying foxes in the Australian city of Melbourne in 2003.

Before the Sydney plan could go into effect, however, the bats had to be healthy enough to make the move. And the noise plan couldn't be carried out during the flying fox breeding season because mothers and their young might get separated during relocation. The noise could also stress females about to give birth. To learn more about the health of the colony, scientists trapped the flying foxes, gave them checkups, and fitted them with radio collars.

After years of legal wrangling and studies to see if the flying foxes were healthy enough to be moved, the botanic gardens got permission to move the colony. In early June 2012, they began broadcasting noise at the flying foxes from noise buggies, hoping the flying foxes would shift their campsite. The entire colony did leave, and as of December 2012, the botanic gardens reported that no flying foxes had returned. So far it seems the noise has kept them away.

So, where did they go?

Nick Edards of Batwatch Australia says some of the flying foxes left the city entirely. The others joined existing flying fox roosts 3 miles (5 km) away in Sydney's Centennial Park and 6 miles (10 km) away in the suburb of Wolli Creek near the airport. This worries Edards because Centennial Park has its own rare native trees that the flying foxes may destroy.

There's another reason Edards is worried. People are bringing a higher than usual number

A WILDLIFE RESCUE WORKER RELEASES A GRAY-HEADED FLYING FOX IN SYDNEY IN 2011. AS A RESULT OF FLOODING THAT YEAR, FLYING FOXES BEGAN LOOKING FOR POLLEN AND NECTAR IN SUBURBAN GARDENS. RESIDENTS PUT UP NETTING TO DISCOURAGE THE STARVING BATS FROM FEEDING ON FRUIT TREES. HOWEVER, THE BATS BECAME TRAPPED IN THE NETTING, REQUIRING A LARGE NUMBER OF BAT RESCUES.

of sick and injured flying foxes to wildlife rehabilitation centers to be nursed back to health and released. Some of the flying foxes have run into power lines or gotten caught in netting or have a disease caused by ticks. It's not clear yet whether moving the flying foxes out of the gardens and the higher number of sick and injured animals are related.

Will the people of Sydney find ways to make room for giant bats in their city? All four species of flying fox in Australia are under pressure as climate warms and the animals' habitat shrinks. If flying foxes are to survive in our warming, urban world, people in Sydney and other cities will have to make difficult choices where there are no easy answers.

CHAPTER 6

THE TURTLE
BY THE BEACH HOUSE

SARASOTA, FLORIDA

IT WAS A WARM SUMMER NIGHT IN 2001 ON GASPARILLA, A TINY BARRIER ISLAND OFF THE COAST OF FLORIDA. ELEVEN-YEAR-OLD ZANDER SRODES WAS ON THE BEACH WITH SOME FRIENDS, SETTING OFF FIREWORKS AFTER DARK. After they had set off a few, they saw a woman approaching across the sand. She went up to Srodes and his friends to let them know that the glow of the fireworks was interfering with nesting loggerhead sea turtles on the beach.

Sea turtles, including loggerheads, are endangered. In fact, sea turtles are among the most endangered animals on Earth. While each female sea turtle lays more than one hundred eggs, only a few will live long enough to reproduce. Experts estimate that there are only 44,500 loggerhead females of nesting age in the entire world. They are at high risk for becoming extinct in the near future.

As part of the effort to help sea turtles, concerned citizens in Florida have permits from the Florida Fish and Wildlife Conservation Commission to survey turtle nests and to rehabilitate sick and injured turtles. Since the late 1990s, Linda Soderquist—the woman on the beach that night—had held the state permit for Gasparilla Island. Srodes recalled the incident ten years later, at a conference for teen leaders called TEDxTeen: "[Linda Soderquist] starts screaming at me about how these lights that I'm shining into the sky are messing with these sea turtles' vision of the moon so they're not going be able to get back down to the water. And so I'm with my friends and being a punk, an eleven-year-old kid, I'm like, 'Get out of here, you know, go home you old lady.' The next morning, I get up and she's in my house, having coffee with my mom."

STAFF WITH THE SEA TURTLE REHABILITATION HOSPITAL AT MOTE MARINE LAB IN SARASOTA RELEASE VALENTINE INTO THE OCEAN AS ONLOOKERS SNAP PHOTOS. THE LOGGERHEAD HAD BEEN STRANDED NEAR NAPLES, FLORIDA, THE MONTH BEFORE AND APPEARED TO BE POISONED AS A RESULT OF LARGE CONCENTRATIONS OF ALGAE IN THE WATER. THESE ALGAE BLOOMS ARE OFTEN THE RESULT OF AGRICULTURAL RUNOFF AND OTHER HUMAN ACTIVITIES. VALENTINE WAS NURSED BACK TO HEALTH AND RELEASED AT A SARASOTA BEACH.

LOGGERHEAD SEA TURTLE FACTS

Loggerheads are named for their wide heads, which have powerful jaws to crack open the crabs they eat. The marine turtles migrate long distances through the ocean, putting them at risk from fishing nets and other human materials

SCIENTIFIC NAME: *Caretta caretta*

ALSO KNOWN AS: Loggerhead is the only English common name.

RELATED TO: Turtles and tortoises, and more distantly to lizards and snakes.

weighing 300 pounds (136 kg)

NATIVE TO FLORIDA: Yes

ENDANGERED: Yes (Loggerheads are listed as Endangered by the International Union for the Conservation of Nature and

TALKING TURTLE

Srodes stayed in his room until Soderquist left, but his mother made him go to Soderquist's house for a talk. Srodes went, expecting to be chewed out by the "old lady." But what he found instead was a woman dedicated to turtles—and equally dedicated to proving to a young punk why turtles mattered and why he should care.

Their friendship would take young Zander Srodes around the world, from his hometown of Placida, Florida, to Costa Rica, Trinidad, Japan, and India. That chance meeting on the beach transformed Srodes's life, turning him into the world's youngest champion of sea turtles and one of its most passionate.

After meeting Soderquist, Srodes started doing Turtle Talks, telling groups of schoolkids his own age about the dangers sea turtles face. "Kids would go home and their parents would say, 'What did you learn in school today?' and the kids would say, 'Well, this guy came to talk to us about sea turtles.'" Srodes spread the word about the dangers sea turtles face from plastic in the ocean and lights on the beach. He told his peers what they could do to help turtles. "No one wakes up in the morning saying, 'How am I going to have a negative impact on sea turtles today,'" he says. By spreading the word through Turtle Talks, Srodes was able to educate kids and their parents and get some of them in areas near nesting sea turtles to turn off lights and to recycle plastics. As a college student these days, Srodes spends his summers traveling, speaking, and sharing his passion for turtles with high school students.

URBAN TURTLES

But why are loggerheads and other sea turtles in trouble? How can fireworks and plastic hurt them? And how are they an example of urban wildlife? As the name implies, sea turtles spend most of their lives in the ocean. They only venture onto beaches to lay their eggs. To walk on land, sea turtles use their paddlelike flippers, which they also use for swimming in the ocean.

Turtles already are threatened by all kinds of human-made dangers in the ocean. They can be hit by a boat's propeller or caught in shrimping nets. Polluted water can make them sick. And turtles can't tell the difference between one of their favorite foods—a squid—and a plastic bag floating in the ocean. If a turtle eats a plastic bag, the bag blocks its digestive system and the turtle will die.

The beach has its own perils. Like all sea turtles, loggerheads must come onto land to lay their eggs. The female uses her flippers to drag her 300-pound (136 kg) body up onto the beach. Above the high-tide mark, where ocean water does not reach, she will dig a nest 2 feet (0.6 m) deep. There she lays about one hundred eggs, each the size and shape of a Ping-Pong ball. After covering her eggs with sand, the mother turtle will return to the ocean.

The problem is that in Florida and around the world, many cities run right up to the beach.

Humans have built hotels and restaurants and houses and parking lots just steps from the water. This means that the turtles have automatically become part of our cities. And our love of living near the ocean is putting loggerheads and other sea turtles in danger.

A DANGEROUS GLOW

Some of the danger is to the nesting turtle mother. She can become entangled in beach furniture or fall into a hole left by a sandcastle. She can become trapped by a seawall or other barrier and starve before she finds her way back to the ocean.

Turtle hatchlings face the greatest danger. Every year in June or July, about sixty days after the mother lays her eggs, little loggerheads will emerge from their shells at night. Only 2 inches (5 cm) long, the hatchling has to dig its way up through the sand. Then it crawls as fast as its tiny flippers can carry it toward the moonlit sea.

That's how it's supposed to be and how it's been for millions of years. But what if the moon isn't the brightest light on the beach? Throughout

LOGGERHEAD TURTLES ARE BORN ON LAND AND RETURN TO THE OCEAN ABOUT SIXTY DAYS AFTER BIRTH. THE TURTLES CAN REMAIN UNDERWATER FOR HOURS BEFORE COMING UP FOR A FEW MINUTES TO BREATHE.

coastal Florida, bright electric lights shine on hotel parking lots; illuminate roadways and sidewalks; light the doorways of beachfront condos; and advertise fast-food restaurants, gas stations, and other all-night businesses.

Baby turtles move toward these artificial lights—and to almost certain death. They're crushed by cars, caught by cats, or they fall down storm drains. Bright artificial lights have even led baby turtles onto a baseball field while a night game was in progress. Sometimes they die from exhaustion as they desperately try to find the ocean.

LIGHTS OUT FOR TURTLES

In 2003 residents of Sarasota, Florida, saw what was happening to sea turtles in their community. At first, volunteers tried placing metal cages around turtle nests to protect them. Then, when the hatchlings were born, volunteers could release them and direct them safely to the water. Volunteers also tried removing eggs from the nest and hatching them in turtle hatcheries. But these efforts didn't do anything about light pollution.

Since then biologists have realized that the problem isn't just with lights along the coast. The problem is that lights as far as 5 miles (8 km) away light up the sky and cause sky glow along Florida's beaches. No matter what people living along the coast did to shade, dim, or turn off their lights, the glow of lighting from communities nowhere near the ocean was affecting nesting turtles in Sarasota.

For this reason, Florida Power and Light is

LIGHT POLLUTION IS A MAJOR THREAT TO URBAN LOGGERHEADS. DRAWN TOWARD HUMAN LIGHTS, TURTLES ARE LURED AWAY FROM THE OCEAN AND TOWARD ROADWAYS AND OTHER DEADLY DANGERS.

helping its customers protect the turtles. The company is suggesting ways for coastal customers to adjust lighting so it's more turtle friendly. This can mean replacing bright light fixtures with bulbs that use a wavelength the turtles can't see or that point light downward. It can also mean installing motion-sensitive timers. Timers help turtles by keeping lights turned off except when people actually trigger them by walking by. Customers can also install dark tinting on windows facing the beach. It all adds up to better lighting for humans but with fewer lights.

DIMMING THE LIGHTS

Palm Beach County is also taking steps to protect the turtles. In May 2012, the county proposed new regulations to create a dim zone. The dim zone would extend from the beaches of Palm Beach, Florida, 3 to 5 miles (5 to 8 km) inland. In the dim zone, businesses would be required to dim or turn off lights at night during the turtle-breeding season. The idea isn't popular, however. Car dealerships argue that they have to be brightly lit at night for customer safety and to protect cars from thieves. Sports stadiums

IS LIGHT POLLUTION MAKING US SICK?

Artificial light takes a toll on many living things. Bright light makes salmon fry (newly hatched fish) seek out the calmer, dimmer water close to shore, where they are eaten by bigger fish. It causes migrating birds to lose their way and crash into buildings. In the 1990s, scientists began to suspect that light pollution didn't just harm individual species. It was harming entire ecosystems. It may even harm human health.

Some researchers report that artificial light may disrupt the human immune system, hampering our ability to fight illnesses. Some even suggest that light pollution may play a role in diseases such as cancer and diabetes. For example, artificial light may be robbing our bodies of the hormone melatonin, which regulates our natural sleep and wake cycles. Our bodies make less of this hormone when we are exposed to bright light. And researchers have observed that melatonin seems to play a role in protecting our cells from changes that can lead to cancer.

argue they have to be brightly lit for night games.

Palm Beach County has rolled out a public education campaign hoping to change Floridians' minds. The message is "Dark Skies Save Sea Turtles' Lives."

A darker sky will be better for the turtles, and it might even be better for us. Will the message get across in time for the turtles?

CHAPTER 7
THE GATOR IN THE TWO-CAR GARAGE

HOUSTON, TEXAS

OVER A FIVE-DAY PERIOD IN JUNE 2012, MORE THAN 15 INCHES (38 CM) OF RAIN FELL ON HOUSTON, TEXAS. THE DOWNPOUR CAUSED MANY CREEKS TO OVERFLOW THEIR BANKS AND FLOODED HUNDREDS OF HOMES. IT ALSO BROUGHT CLOUDS OF MOSQUITOES AND SOMETHING WITH A BIGGER BITE: ALLIGATORS.

The heavy spring rains had created a system of watery highways, and alligators are most at home in the water. They used the new water highways to move around more freely—and they ended up in the city. Biologist Louise Hayes-Odum explains that in the spring, young alligators called subadults leave their mothers to look for territory to call their own. These subadults, which are 3 to 6 feet (1 to 1.8 m) long, spread out from where they hatched and begin to look for mates.

In June 2012, roaming gators followed the water highways into Houston neighborhoods such as the Heights. One homeowner there found a 6.5-foot (2 m) gator in her garage!

HOUSTON, TEXAS, IS KNOWN AS THE BAYOU CITY FOR ITS MANY MILES OF SLOW-MOVING STREAMS, WHERE ALLIGATORS LIVE. IN 2012 HEAVY SPRING RAIN (*ABOVE*) DREW MANY OF THESE BAYOU GATORS INTO THE CITY.

PEOPLE OFTEN CONFUSE ALLIGATORS *(BELOW)* WITH CROCODILES. AN EASY WAY TO DISTINGUISH THE TWO REPTILES IS TO LOOK AT THE ANIMAL'S SNOUT. IF IT'S U-SHAPED, IT'S AN ALLIGATOR. IF IT'S V-SHAPED, YOU'RE LOOKING AT A CROCODILE.

ALLIGATOR FACTS

One of North America's largest reptiles, the alligator prefers freshwater lakes, ponds, and rivers. It hunts waterbirds, fish, and turtles in the water and can drag in and kill a deer, nutria (a semiaquatic rodent), or other mammal that comes to the water's edge to drink.

SCIENTIFIC NAME: **Alligator mississippiensis**

ALSO KNOWN AS: American alligator, Florida alligator, Mississippi alligator, Louisiana alligator

RELATED TO: Caimans and crocodiles

SIZE: Females average about 9 feet (3 m). Males are about 13 feet (4 m). An adult alligator can weigh up to 1,000 pounds (453 kg).

NATIVE TO NORTH AMERICA: Yes

ENDANGERED: No (Alligators are listed as Threatened due to Similarity of Appearance on the U.S. Endangered Species List so hunters don't confuse the alligator with its endangered look-alike, the American crocodile.)

Alligators hadn't suddenly invaded. The ancestors of modern alligators were in Texas long before the arrival of Europeans. The Atakapa tribe from southeastern Texas revered the alligator.

When they did kill the animal, they used every part of its body, even using its fat to make bug repellent.

In the twenty-first century, most Houstonians don't hold the gator in such high regard. Animal control officers and professional nuisance-alligator wranglers in Houston have been called to retrieve alligators from golf courses, cemeteries, schoolyards, and porches in the city and its suburbs. They try to relocate the gators to the bayous (slow-moving streams) where the animals usually live. But if the gators return to the city, they are killed.

BACK FROM THE BRINK

Once an endangered species, alligators were protected from hunting in Texas, starting in 1969. This allowed the wild gator population to grow, and the American alligator became a conservation success story. By 1984 the species had recovered so much that the State of Texas began allowing hunting again. Just to be safe, Texas listed the species as Threatened Due to Similarity of Appearance, because it looked a lot like the highly endangered crocodile.

Then, as coastal development boomed in the 1990s, alligators were squeezed out of their habitat. Texas had more people (about 18 million in the mid-1990s) and more alligators (half a million) than ever before, and they were living closer to each other.

Take the case of Sienna Plantation, population fourteen thousand. It's a 7,000-acre (2,800-hectare) community in Missouri City, Texas, not too far from Houston. Sienna Plantation has a golf club, a water park, soccer and baseball fields, eight tennis courts, thirty-six parks—and

THE ALLIGATOR CAPITOL OF TEXAS

About 50 miles (80 km) east of downtown Houston is Anahuac, the Alligator Capitol of Texas. Every year this town of twenty-two hundred hosts Gatorfest: four days of live music, food (including barbecued gator), airboat rides, and the crowning of gator royalty from among local applicants. Between the barbecue contest and a gator roundup, Texas Parks and Wildlife runs an education booth, where staff members give young and old alike a chance to touch a real, live alligator.

MISS GATORFEST WITH A GATOR JAW. ALLIGATORS HAVE ABOUT EIGHTY TEETH, WHICH THEY USE FOR GRASPING AND HOLDING ON TO PREY.

WELCOME, BUT MIND THE ALLIGATORS

Back in 2009 in Pearland, Texas (population ninety thousand), alligators had become so unafraid of people that they took to strolling the sidewalks. In 2012 one gator stopped traffic on the Pearland Parkway. One part of the city even put up fancy green "Beware of Alligators" signs. The Pearland Parks & Recreation Department posts "Alligator Safety Tips" on its website, including these: "Don't tease the gators, don't feed the gators, and if you hear an alligator hiss, you're too close."

GATORS ARE SO COMMON IN SOME PARTS OF TEXAS THAT CITIZENS PUT UP WARNING SIGNS *(FAR LEFT)* NEAR PONDS AND OTHER BODIES OF WATER THAT ATTRACT THE ANIMALS.

about two hundred resident gators. The Sienna Plantation community was landscaped to include trails, parks, and lakes for kayaking and fishing. This was ideal gator habitat.

During the heavy spring rains of 2012, the alligators got active. In one ten-day span, a professional trapper removed twenty-one gators from Sienna Plantation. One 11-foot (3 m) animal was caught not far from Sienna Crossing Elementary, a school with nearly one thousand students. The school's mascot? The gator.

BITING THE HAND THAT FEEDS IT

When alligators and humans share the same space, it's often human behavior that causes problems. For example, gators like to climb onto the banks of a waterway to warm up in the sun. At the first sign of a human, a wild gator will slip quietly and quickly into the water. But when people clean fish and throw the scraps into the water, they teach gators to associate people with food. Sometimes thrill seekers will feed gators on purpose, to get a closer look and bragging rights. This is illegal—and incredibly dangerous. Feeding gators can make them unafraid and aggressive: a deadly combination. Wildlife experts agree that the biggest threat from alligators comes when they lose their shyness of people.

Each year, Texas Parks and Wildlife signs up about fifty licensed hunters to go after nuisance gators. These are the animals that kill pets or livestock or that pose a threat to human safety. Most male nuisance gators are trapped and shot on the spot. Female nuisance gators may be brought to alligator farms to be bred. Farmed gators are used in tourist shows, for meat, and for leather to make into belts, purses, and cowboy boots.

For the residents of Houston, the best weapon against gators may prove to be greater understanding and appreciation of these amazing creatures—and a lot of caution and common sense. Nuisance alligators aren't hatched. They're made.

EPILOGUE

WHILE WRITING THIS BOOK, I READ ABOUT MANY OTHER URBAN SPECIES: VULTURES IN NEW DELHI, INDIA; WILD BOARS IN BERLIN, GERMANY; AND AFRICAN PENGUINS IN CAPE TOWN, SOUTH AFRICA. The map on pages 54–55 highlights some of these animals for you to explore on your own. Countless species live alongside us in suburbs and cities the world over. And in the coming decades, people and wildlife will continue to be squeezed closer and closer together. The United Nations projects that 67 percent of humanity will live in urban areas by the year 2050. The projected figure for some countries is even higher. By 2050 some population experts think that 90 percent of the U.S. population will live in a city or its suburbs.

As this high-rise, glassed-in, paved-over environment becomes the main landscape on every inhabited continent, we will drive many species to extinction. Those that survive will be forced to make their livings among us, in our cities. Will we see them as pests and nuisances to be removed, or will we adapt ourselves and see them as our wild animal neighbors? Can we design the cities of the future to be a safe home for wildlife too?

A HEALTHY PLANET HAS LOTS OF SPECIES

These are important questions, because adapting cities to make room for wildlife may be the only way to preserve what biodiversity we have left. And scientists believe biodiversity is key to our own species' survival.

The natural world provides us with the air we breathe and the food and water we need to survive. Plants turn the energy of the sun into a form of energy we can use. They also provide us with sources of food, fuel, and medicines. From tiny bacteria to giant whales, animal species—including humans—are interconnected in complex webs. When a species goes extinct, unpredictable consequences can follow. For example, viruses that cause disease live in host species. The viruses can jump from one species to another one and into people. When there are a lot of different animal species to serve as hosts for a virus, it is much less likely to make the jump into human hosts. But when there are fewer host species, the risk of a human disease outbreak from viruses goes up.

MAKING CHOICES, RAISING VOICES

We can do many things—as individuals, as communities, and as a nation—to reduce the size of humanity's footprint. To save the species with whom we share this planet means living every day thoughtfully and keeping the consequences of our actions in mind. Whether to bike or take the car, what to eat and how to grow it, what to buy and what to throw away: all these choices will affect the kind of world we will inhabit in 2015, 2025, and 2050. Chances are it will be a warmer world, with more people, and fewer species. We can imagine a different world, but we have to work to make that vision happen.

Designing cities for both people and wildlife is an important part of that vision. Citizens who share this vision have to speak up to urge city planners to include and pay for the needs of wildlife in their designs. We have to be noisy, and we have to make our voices heard. We have to speak for our wild animal neighbors.

HUMANS AND WILDLIFE INTERSECT IN URBAN AREAS ALL OVER THE WORLD. IN THIS PHOTO, PEDESTRIANS IN GDYNIA, POLAND, WATCH A FAMILY OF WILD BOARS STROLLING ALONG THE COAST OF THE BALTIC SEA.

BOULDER BEACH IN CAPE TOWN, SOUTH AFRICA, IS A FAMOUS SPOT FOR GETTING CLOSE TO AFRICAN PENGUINS (BELOW). HOWEVER, THE PENGUINS ARE WANDERING INTO THE BACKYARDS OF HOMES THAT LIE NEAR THE BEACH AND ARE DESTROYING GARDENS AND LEAVING SMELLY DROPPINGS BEHIND.

URBAN WILDLIFE

moose
Anchorage, Alaska

NORTH AMERICA

turkey & black vultures
Wenonah, New Jersey •

ATLANTIC OCEAN

PACIFIC OCEAN

SOUTH AMERICA

sloths
Rio de Janeiro, Brazil •

The human population on Earth has reached more than seven billion people. As that number increases, wildlife habitat is increasingly reduced through human development. Wildlife sightings in urban areas are therefore increasingly common. This map offers some examples of wild animals around the globe that have moved into cities. Learn more about them by checking Encyclopedia of Life (eol.org), ARKive (arkive.org), and eNature (enature.com).

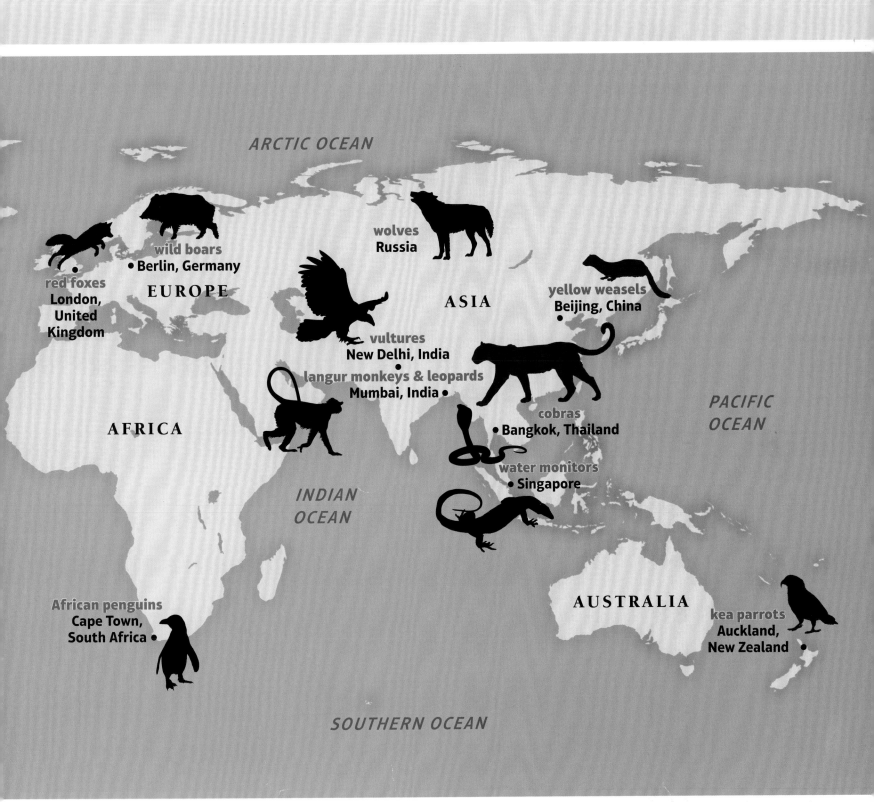

ARCTIC OCEAN

red foxes
London,
United
Kingdom

wild boars
• Berlin, Germany

EUROPE

wolves
Russia

ASIA

yellow weasels
Beijing, China

vultures
New Delhi, India

langur monkeys & leopards
Mumbai, India •

AFRICA

cobras
• Bangkok, Thailand

PACIFIC
OCEAN

INDIAN
OCEAN

water monitors
• Singapore

African penguins
Cape Town,
South Africa •

AUSTRALIA

kea parrots
Auckland,
New Zealand

SOUTHERN OCEAN

A BIOCITY IN BRAZIL

What would a wildlife-friendly city look like? It might resemble Curitiba, a city of 1.7 million on the southern coast of Brazil. It's widely considered one of the most livable cities in the world for people. Curitiba has 2 square miles (5 sq. km) of green space for every inhabitant, its city bus system is one of the best public transportation systems of any large urban area, and residents recycle 70 percent of their waste.

This huge metropolitan area has an astonishing variety of wildlife. In addition to snakes and frogs, Curitiba is home to two hundred species of birds and thirty-seven types of mammals, including deer, otters, capybaras (a tailless rodent), armadillos, and agoutis (a rodent the size of a rabbit). Yet Curitiba's wildlife was still losing habitat as people on the city outskirts cleared remaining forests and drained wetlands. So in 2007, the city launched the Biocidade (Biocity) program to preserve remaining habitat, to plant native trees in the city, and to educate citizens about biodiversity. Ongoing projects include surveying the tiny invertebrates (spineless creatures such as crayfish, mussels, and insect larvae) that live in the streams, rivers, and lakes in and around Curitiba. Clean waterways teeming with prey can encourage birds and mammals to return to previously polluted areas.

HOW GREEN IS YOUR CITY?

Residents of Berne, Switzerland, are speaking up. There, city planners are experimenting with green roofs that won't just provide homes for insects. They will also be home to ground-nesting birds such as endangered plovers and lapwings. Green roofs are planted with vegetation that appeals to a range of animals. The rooftop plants do all kinds of good things. They remove carbon dioxide and pollutants from the air, lower the cost of heating and cooling the building, and help cool the city. In Birmingham, England, efforts are under way to provide green roofs for the endangered redstart. Green roofs are sprouting up in cities across the United States too, including at the Ford Motor plant in Dearborn, Michigan; at a library in Seattle, Washington; and at City Hall in Chicago, Illinois.

In the city of Toronto, Ontario, in Canada, the Evergreen Brick Works project restored a former brick quarry into a park and a nature reserve. The design includes a pond to capture storm water. The pond will eventually provide a wetland for birds, frogs, and other wildlife. Native plants in a bird thicket will attract birds, butterflies, and

THE EVERGREEN BRICK WORKS IS AN URBAN RENEWAL PROJECT IN TORONTO, ONTARIO. IT RESTORED AN OLD QUARRY INTO A GREEN SPACE FOR URBAN WILDLIFE IN THE HEART OF DOWNTOWN TORONTO.

IN SEOUL, SOUTH KOREA—A CITY OF MORE THAN 10 MILLION PEOPLE—URBAN LEADERS WORKED TO BRING MORE GREEN SPACE INTO THE CITY. FAMILIES ENJOY THE COOLING WATERS OF CHEONGGYECHEON STREAM IN DOWNTOWN SEOUL.

other pollinators. Trees have been planted to help cool the area to reduce the heat island effect (the amount of heat a city traps). The reserve also includes an education center for teaching the citizens of Toronto how to live more sustainably.

In South Korea, the city of Seoul demolished an overhead highway built in the 1960s. The city also restored its historic Cheonggyecheon waterway, creating a beautiful green oasis in the center of the city. Since work began on the Cheonggyecheon project in 2003, species biodiversity in the city has increased sixfold. For example, birds, mammals, reptiles, fish, frogs,

and other wildlife have begun to return. The restoration project has also reduced the heat island effect. Removing the elevated highway reduced car traffic and lowered air pollution.

Humans are the dominant species on Earth. Working together, we have perfected technology to transform the surface of our planet. But that transformation and our modern way of life have come at a dreadful cost for wildlife. Will we use all our intelligence and resourcefulness to shape an urban world where both people and other living things can survive?

SOURCE NOTES

12 City of Santa Monica, CA, e-mail, quoted in Kevin Roderick, "Mountain Lions Spotted in Santa Monica, Griffith Park," *Laobserved.com*, May 22, 2012, http://www.laobserved.com/archive/2012/05/mountain_lions_spotted_in.php (December 2, 2012).

17 Ryan Bourbour, e-mail to the author, October 31, 2012.

17 Breanna Martinico, e-mail to the author, November 12, 2012.

17 Bourbour, e-mail.

20 Shintaro Ishihara, quoted in Blaine Harden, "In Tokyo, Hitchcock Isn't Around but He Seems to Have Sent the Birds," *Washingtonpost.com*, July 26, 2009, http://www.washingtonpost.com/wp-dyn/content/article/2009/07/25/AR2009072502170.html (January 6, 2013).

33 Stanley Gehrt, e-mail to the author, October 9, 2012.

33 Ibid.

36 Peggy Eby, speech, meeting of the Bat-Human Project, Cook and Philip Park, Sydney, Australia, April 29, 2001, video transcribed by author, available online at http://vimeo.com/29341700 (December 16, 2012).

36–37 Ibid.

40 Zander Srodes, "The Moment It Found Me," speech, TEDxTeen 2011, New York, April 2, 2011, available online as a YouTube video, 5:49, http://www.youtube.com/watch?v=hZR214wjIfA (October 23, 2012).

42 Zander Srodes, phone conversation with the author, October 24, 2012.

42 Ibid.

SELECTED BIBLIOGRAPHY

Adamski, Katrina. "Flying Foxes Drive Residents Batty." *North Shore Times*, July 3, 2009. http://north-shore-times.whereilive.com.au/news/story/flying-foxes-drive-residents-batty/ (October 11, 2012).

Associated Press. "1st Cape Cod Bear Captures Residents' Imaginations." *Usatoday.com*. June 7, 2012. http://usatoday30.usatoday.com/news/nation/story/2012-06-07/cape-cod-bear/55450090/1 (October 26, 2012).

Australian Associated Press. "Flying Foxes to Stay in Historic Gardens." *Sydney Morning Herald*, June 22, 2010.

Chicago Tribune. "So This Coyote Walks into a Quiznos… No Joke: Sightings Spike This Time of Year in Chicago." *Chicagotribune.com*, April 4, 2007. http://articles.chicagotribune.com/2007-04-04/news/0704040747_1_coyote-anne-kent-bina-patel (December 5, 2012).

Couser, Dorothy. "Atakapa Indians." *Handbook of Texas Online*. Texas State Historical Association. N.d. http://www.tshaonline.org/handbook/online/articles/bma48 (October 30, 2012).

Department of Economic and Social Affairs, Population Division. "World Urbanization Prospects: The 2011 Revision. Highlights." New York: United Nations, 2012.

Fackler, M. "Japan Fights Crowds of Crows." *Kagoshima Journal. Nytimes.com*, May 7, 2008. http://www.nytimes.com/2008/05/07/world/asia/07crows.html?pagewanted=all (March 2, 2012).

Fleming, Susan K. *A Murder of Crows*. DVD. Hollywood, CA: PBS Home Video/Paramount Home Entertainment, 2010. Also available online at http://www.pbs.org/wnet/nature/episodes/a-murder-of-crows/full-episode/5977/ (February 5, 2013).

———. *Raccoon Nation*. DVD. Hollywood, CA: PBS Home Video/Paramount Home Entertainment, 2011. Also available online at http://www.pbs.org/wnet/nature/episodes/raccoon-nation/full-episode/7558/ (February 5, 2013).

Freemantle, Tony. "Alligators Popping Up in the Houston Area." *Houston Chronicle*, April 13, 2012. http://www.chron.com/news/houston-texas/article/Gators-looking-for-love-in-a-neighborhood-near-you-3481534.php (October 7, 2012).

Gehrt, Stanley D. "Ecology and Management of Striped Skunks, Raccoons, and Coyotes in Urban Landscapes." In *People and Predators: From Conflict to Coexistence*, edited by Nina Fascione, Aimee Delach, and Martin Smith, 81-104. Washington, DC: Island Press, 2004.

Gehrt, Stanley D., and Seth P. D. Riley. "Coyotes (*Canis latrans*)." In *Urban Carnivores: Ecology, Conflict, and Conservation*, edited by Stanley D. Gehrt, Seth P. D. Riley, and Brian L. Cypher, 79–95. Baltimore: Johns Hopkins University Press, 2010.

Hadidian, John, Suzanne Prange, Richard Rosatte, Seth P. D. Riley, and Stanley D. Gehrt. "Raccoons (*Procyon lotor*)." In *Urban Carnivores: Ecology, Conflict, and Conservation*, edited by Stanley D., Gehrt, Seth P. D. Riley, and Brian L. Cypher, 35-48. Baltimore: Johns Hopkins University Press, 2010.

Hall, Leslie, and Greg Richards. *Flying Foxes: Fruit and Blossom Bats of Australia*. Australian Natural History series. Malabar, FL: Kreiger Publishing, 2000.

Harden, Blaine. In "Tokyo, Hitchcock Isn't Around, but He Seems to Have Sent the Birds." *Washingtonpost.com*, July 26, 2009. http://www.washingtonpost.com/wp-dyn /content/article/2009/07/25/AR2009072502170.html (March 2, 2012).

Hayes-Odum, Louise. Personal communication with author. October 28, 2012.

Iwaniuk, Andrew N. "The Evolution of Skilled Forelimb Movements in Carnivorans." Thesis. University of Lethbridge, 2000.

Jennings, Angel. "Mountain Lion Killed in Santa Monica Was Probably Seeking a Home." *Latimes.com*, May 24, 2012. http://articles.latimes.com/2012/may/24/local/la-me-0524-mountain-lion-20120524 (December 19, 2012).

Johnson, John. "Whip-Smart and Curious, Raccoons Are Resilient Urban Residents." *Seattletimes.com*, July 30, 2004. http://community.seattletimes.nwsource.com /archive/?date=20040730&slug=raccoons30 (December 19, 2012).

Keller, Dawn. "Coyote Returns to the Wild." *Flint Creek Wildlife Rehabilitation* (blog), April 5, 2007. http://www .flintcreekwildlife.org/blog/coyote_returns_to_the_wild/ (December 6, 2012).

Krasny, Ros. "Wandering Cape Cod Bear Captured in Boston Suburb." *Reuters.com,* June 27, 2012. http://www.reuters.com/article/2012/06/27/us-usa-blackbear-boston-idUSBRE85Q08920120627 (October 26, 2012).

Kurosawa, R., R. Kono, T. Kondo, and Y. Kanai. "Diet of Jungle Crows in an Urban Landscape." *Global Environmental Research* 7, no. 2 (2003):193–198.

Lindsey, Fredrica. "Saving Sea Turtles with a Lights-Out Policy in Florida." *National Geographic News*, March 10, 2003. http://news.nationalgeographic.com/news/2003/03/0310_030310_turtlelight.html (September 11, 2012).

"Major Implications of the Study: What We Learned." The Cook County, Illinois, Coyote Project. N.d. http://www.urbancoyoteresearch.com/The_Results_Of_The_Study.htm (December 6, 2012).

Marine Turtle Specialist Group. *Caretta caretta.* IUCN Red List of Threatened Species. Version 2012.2. http://www.iucnredlist.org/details/3897/0. (October 23, 2012).

MassWildlife. "Black Bears in Massachusetts." Living with Bears Page. September 11, 2012. http://www.mass.gov/dfwele/dfw/wildlife/living/living_with_bears.htm (October 14, 2012).

Mulvaney, Erin. "Nearly 6-foot Gator Caught in Heights Garage." *Houston Chronicle*, July 17, 2012. http://www.chron.com/news/houston-texas/article/Nearly-6-foot-gator-caught-in-Heights-garage-3714537.php (October 7, 2012).

"Our Packs." The Cook County, Illinois, Coyote Project. N.d. http://www.urbancoyoteresearch.com/OurPacks.htm (December 6, 2012).

Reid, Andy, and Susannah Bryan. "Saving Sea Turtles Could Mean Lowered Lights—Miles from Shore." *South Florida Sun Sentinel*, May 28, 2012. http://articles.sun-sentinel.com/2012-05-28/news/fl-broward-sea-turtle-light-fight-20120528_1_richard-whitecloud-sea-turtles-bright-lights (October 23, 2012).

Rich, Catherine, and Travis Longcore, eds. *The Ecological Consequences of Artificial Lighting*. Washington, DC: Island Press, 2005.

Riley, Seth, and Jeff Sikich. Phone conversation with author, 2012.

Royal Botanic Gardens and Domain Trust. Flying Foxes: Frequently Asked Questions Page. N.d. http://www.rbgsyd.nsw.gov.au/welcome/royal_botanic_garden/gardens_and_domain/wildlife/flying-foxes (October 11, 2012).

Ruediger, Bill. "Carnivore Conservation and Highways: Understanding the Relationships, Problems, and Solutions." In *People and Predators: From Conflict to Coexistence*, edited by Nina Fascione, Aimee Delach, and Martin Smith, 132-150. Washington, DC: Island Press, 2004.

Witherington, Blair E., and R. Erik Martin. "Understanding, Assessing, and Resolving Light-Pollution Problems on Sea Turtle Nesting Beaches." Florida Marine Research Institute. Technical Report, TR-2. St. Petersburg: Florida Marine Research Institute, 2000.

Zeveloff, Samuel. *Raccoons: A Natural History*. Vancouver: UBC Press, 2002.

FOR FURTHER INFORMATION

BOOKS

Bosselaar, Laure-Anne. *Urban Nature: Poems about Wildlife in the City*. Minneapolis: Milkweed Editions, 2000.

Feigenbaum, Aaron. *American Alligators: Freshwater Survivors*. America's Animal Comebacks series. New York: Bearport Publishing, 2008.

Feinstein, Julie. *A Field Guide to Urban Wildlife: Common Animals of Cities & Suburbs and How They Adapt and Thrive*. Mechanicsburg, PA: Stackpole Books, 2011.

Fenton, Brock. *Bats*. Markham, ON: Fitzhenry & Whiteside, 2012.

Hickman, Pamela. *Turtle Rescue: Changing the Future for Endangered Wildlife*. Richmond Hill, ON: Firefly Books, 2005.

Hodgkins, Fran. *Animals Among Us: Living with Suburban Wildlife*. New Haven, CT: Linnet Books, 2000.

Johnson, Sylvia A. *Crows*. Nature Watch series. Minneapolis: Lerner Publications, 2005.

Markle, Sandra. *Mountain Lions*. Animal Predators series. Minneapolis: Lerner Publications, 2010.

Read, Nicholas. *City Critters: Wildlife in the Urban Jungle*. Victoria, BC: Orca Book Publishers, 2012.

Read, Tracy. *Exploring the World of Coyotes*. Richmond Hill, ON: Firefly Books, 2011.

———. *Exploring the World of Raccoons*. Richmond Hill, ON: Firefly Books, 2010.

Swinburne, Stephen R. *Black Bear: North America's Bear*. Honesdale, PA: Boyd's Mills Press, 2009.

WEBSITES

Audubon Society's Healthy Yard Pledge
http://www.audubon.org/healthy-yard-pledge-0
Enlist your family in conserving water, reducing pesticide use, removing invasive plants, and planting native species that will attract birds, bees, and butterflies.

Celebrate Urban Birds Project
http://www.birds.cornell.edu/celebration/
Take part in the Cornell Laboratory of Ornithology's Celebrate Urban Birds project. This project enlists kids across North America and the world as citizen scientists. Learn to identify city birds, take part in real research, or apply for a mini grant to fund a project in your own neighborhood, no matter where you live.

Encyclopedia of Life
http://www.flickr.com/groups/encyclopedia_of_life/
Share your images of urban wildlife with the Encyclopedia of Life (EOL). This ambitious global project is creating a Web page for each species on the planet. You can upload images to the EOL group Flickr pool. Experts will verify your image and add it to the proper species page. You can also find other ways to participate in the EOL project on its website at eol.org.

iNaturalist
http://www.inaturalist.org
This site is a social network for naturalists. Using the iNaturalist smartphone app, you can upload sightings of urban wildlife to this global, online database or search to find species others have reported near you. The app maps your observation, and members of the iNaturalist community can help identify species in your own sightings.

SciStarter
http://www.scistarter.com
Do you want to be a citizen scientist and participate in real science projects? This website can match you with an ongoing project. Pick an activity or a topic through the site's Project Finder to learn more about projects such as the Roadkill Survey for Road Bikers, Project Squirrel, and BeakGeek that might interest you.

INDEX

PHOTO ACKNOWLEDGMENTS

The images in this book are used with the permission of: © Laura Westlund/Independent Picture Service (animal tracks), pp. 54–55 (map); © iStockphoto.com/ryan burke (tire tracks); AP Photo/Tony Gutierrez, p. 1; © Isselee/Dreamstime.com, p. 3; AP Photo/Boston Herald/Mark Garfinkel, pp. 4–5; © iStockphoto.com/Terraxplorer, pp. 6–7; © blickwinkel/Meyers/Alamy, p. 8; © Minden Pictures/SuperStock, p. 9; © Bill Draker/imagebroker/CORBIS, p. 10; © Della Huff/Alamy, p. 12; © Felix Adamo/ZUMA Press/CORBIS, p. 13; AFP/Getty Images/Newscom, p. 14; AP Photo/UC Davis, p. 15; © Michael Macor/San Francisco Chronicle/CORBIS, p. 16; © Sylvain Grandadam/age fotostock/SuperStock, p. 18; AP Photo/The Missoulian, Kurt Wilson, p. 19; © C.S. Ling/Aurora/Getty Images, p. 20; © Allan Baxter/The Image Bank/Getty Images, p. 21; © Ko Sasaki/The New York Times/Redux, pp. 22, 25; © 2007 Jenni Sophia Fuchs/Flickr/Getty Images, p. 23; © Mark P. van Veen/Hollandse Hoogte/Redux, p. 24; © Paolo Patrizi/Alamy, p. 27; AP Photo/AP Photo/Sun-Times, Scott Stewart, p. 29; Mary Evans/Ronald Grant/Everett Collection, p. 30; © Cybernesco/Dreamstime.com, p. 32; AP Photo/Mark Baker, p. 35; © Radius Images/CORBIS, p. 37; AP Photo/Rob Griffith, p. 39; AP Photo/Sarasota Herald-Tribune, E. Skylar Litherland, p. 41; © Lynda Richardson/CORBIS, p. 43; © Delmas Lehman/Dreamstime.com, p. 44; AP Photo/Houston Chronicle, Melissa Phillip, p. 46; © Animals Animals/SuperStock, p. 47; Tom Salyer Stock Connection Worldwide/Newscom, p. 48; Joyce Marshall/KRT/Newscom, p. 49; Photo courtesy of the author, p. 50; AP Photo/Czarek Sokolowski, p. 53 (top); © Brooks Kraft/Sygma/CORBIS, p. 53 (bottom); © CharlineXia Ontario Canada Collection/Alamy, pp. 56–57; © 2011 Renan Gicquel/Flickr/Getty Images, p. 57 (right).

Front cover: © Yva Momatiuk & John Eastcott/Minden Pictures/CORBIS (main); © iStockphoto.com/Terraxplorer (cityscape); © iStockphoto.com/ryan burke (tire tracks); © Laura Westlund/Independent Picture Service (animal tracks).

Back cover: © iStockphoto.com/Terraxplorer (cityscape); © iStockphoto.com/ryan burke (tire tracks); © Laura Westlund/Independent Picture Service (animal tracks).

Main body text set in ITC Berkeley Oldstyle Std Book 10/14

Typeface provided by International Typeface Corp

ABOUT THE AUTHOR

Ann Downer is the author of ten books for young readers, both fiction and nonfiction, including the Hatching Magic series and the award-winning *Elephant Talk: The Surprising Science of Elephant Communication.* She also edits books about science for adults. She lives in Somerville, Massachusetts, with her husband and son.

Expand learning beyond the printed book. Download free, complementary educational resources for this book from our website, www.lerneresource.com.